FAVOURITE PEAK DISTRICT RECIPES

compiled by
Ann Wall

By Dove's fair waters let me stray;
Where Derwent cleaves its rocky way;
Where Haddon's glades half-hidden lie
Beside the bright, meandering Wye.

SALMON

Index

Cover pictures *front:* Miller's Dale *by E. W. Haslehust* RI
back: On the Derwent, Baslow *by W. Biscombe Gardner*
Title page: South Church Street, Bakewell *by E. W. Haslehust* RI

Printed and Published by J. Salmon Ltd., Sevenoaks, England © Copyright

Bakewell Pudding

*This recipe first happened by mistake, when the cook at the Rutland Arms, Bakewell put
the egg mixture on top of the jam instead of on the pastry for a special strawberry tart.
The Bakewell Pudding Shop claims to be the sole purveyor of the authentic pudding,
with the recipe handed down only to members of the family.*

8 oz puff pastry

FILLING
Strawberry jam   4 oz butter, softened   4 oz sugar
4 egg yolks   2 egg whites, beaten   Almond essence

Set oven to 425°F or Mark 7. Grease a wide shallow dish or pie plate. Roll
out the pastry on a floured surface and line the plate. Spread the pastry with
a thick layer of strawberry jam. Cream the butter and sugar together in a
bowl, mix in the egg yolks, the beaten egg whites and the almond essence.
Spread this egg mixture over the jam in the dish. Bake for 15 minutes and then
reduce oven to 350°F or Mark 4 for 20 minutes more cooking. The filling is
meant to remain soft and is not intended to set.

Chatsworth from the Bridge

Derbyshire Fruit Loaf

Mixed with hot tea, this fruit cake will keep well.

1 lb mixed dried fruit	**1 lb self-raising flour**
8 oz sugar	**½ teaspoon mixed spice**
½ pint hot tea (no milk)	**½ teaspoon grated nutmeg**
1 egg	**2 tablespoons marmalade**

Put the dried fruit and the sugar into a mixing bowl, add the hot tea and leave to soak overnight. Next day, set oven to 300°F or Mark 2. Grease and line a 7-inch cake tin or two 1 lb loaf tins. Stir the egg, flour, spices and the marmalade into the fruit, sugar and tea mixture. Pour into the cake tin or the loaf tins. Bake for 1½-2 hours until firm to the touch and a skewer inserted into the cake comes out clean. Do not open the oven during the first hour of baking time. Turn out on to a wire rack to cool.

Easy Chocolate Fudge

No cooking is needed to make this sweet. Condensed, evaporated or fresh milk can be used instead of cream.

4 oz plain chocolate   **3 tablespoons fresh single cream**
2 oz butter   **1 teaspoon vanilla essence**
1 lb icing sugar

Butter an 8-inch square tin. Break the chocolate into pieces and put with the butter into a basin set over a pan of hot water. Leave until the mixture has melted, stirring once or twice. Remove the basin from the pan of water and stir in the cream and the vanilla essence. Gradually mix in the icing sugar. Transfer the mixture to the tin, leave to cool and then cut into squares. Alternatively, keep the mixture soft in a basin over a pan of hot water, off the stove. Take teaspoons of the mixture, roll into balls in hands dusted with icing sugar and dip into dishes of desiccated coconut, chopped nuts, powdered drinking chocolate or 'hundreds and thousands'.

Sausage Plait

Rather like a large, decorative sausage roll,
the plait is cut into slices and served hot or cold.

8 oz shortcrust pastry

FILLING
8 oz sausage meat   2 tomatoes, skinned   1 small onion   2 oz mushrooms
Pinch of mixed herbs   Salt and pepper   1 egg, beaten

Set oven to 400°F or Mark 6. Grease a baking sheet. First skin the tomatoes by immersing in boiling water and peeling. Chop the tomatoes, onion and mushrooms and mix with the sausage meat and the herbs. Roll out the pastry on a floured surface to a rectangle 12 inches by 9 inches and place on the baking sheet. Arrange the filling down the centre of the pastry. Cut the pastry into ½ inch strips at an angle, either side of the filling. Fold the pastry strips, alternately, over the mixture to look like a plait. Brush with beaten egg and bake for 30 to 35 minutes. Serves 4.

Poor Man's Goose

The texture and flavour of this dish is said to be like that of roast goose. No exact quantities can be given as it is a 'poor man's dish', made with whatever is available. Cheese and sliced onion can be used instead of liver.

1 large cooking apple	4 oz liver, sliced
2 teaspoons sugar	1 lb potatoes, sliced
1 packet sage and onion stuffing	Salt and pepper
Dripping	

Set oven to 350°F or Mark 4. Take a deep dish and put a few knobs of dripping in the base. Peel, core and slice the apples and arrange in a layer on the dripping. Sprinkle with the sugar. Make up the sage and onion stuffing as the instructions on the packet and add a layer to the dish, followed by slices of liver. Finally add a layer of raw potatoes cut into slices with a little seasoning. If the dish is deep enough to repeat the layers, finish with a potato layer. Dot with dripping and bake for 1 hour.

The Peak Castle and Cavern, Castleton

Chaddesden Barley Water

A refreshing soft drink for hot summer days.

1 tablespoon pearl barley **8 lumps of sugar**
Peel of 4 lemons   **4 pints boiling water**

Scald the pearl barley by pouring boiling water over it and then strain and discard the water. Put the scalded barley into a large basin with the peel of the 4 lemons cut into strips and the 8 lumps of sugar. Pour 4 pints of boiling water over the barley mixture, cover and leave to cool. When cold, pour slowly into a jug to leave behind the sediment but do not strain it off. The juice of a lemon may be added before serving.

Baked Gammon in Cider

Prime lean, meaty middle gammon sweetened with golden syrup and sugar and baked in cider with tinned peaches.

1 middle gammon or slipper joint	2 tablespoons Demerara sugar
2 bay leaves	½ pint cider
2 teaspoons cloves	1 tin peach halves
2 tablespoons golden syrup	Chopped chives

Total cooking time: allow 20 minutes per pound plus 20 minutes extra. Wash the joint, place in a saucepan, cover with water, add the bay leaves and bring to the boil. Cover and simmer for half the total cooking time. Remove from the pan and discard the liquid. Set oven to 375°F or Mark 5. Remove the skin from the joint, score the fat and press in the cloves. Place in a roasting tin, pour the syrup over the fatty sides and sprinkle with the sugar. Add ½ pint cider to the tin and bake for the remainder of the cooking time. Baste with the liquid 2 or 3 times during cooking. Twenty minutes before the end of cooking time add the drained peach halves, reserving the juice, and sprinkle with chopped chives. When cooked, remove the joint and the peaches to a serving dish. Add the peach juice to the tin and boil rapidly to reduce to make a sauce; serve separately.

Tissington Hall

Salmon Mousse

*This delicious creamy fish mould may be served as an hors d'œuvre with toast
or as a main course with a fresh, green salad.*

1 lb fresh salmon
Bunch fresh herbs or bouquet garni
½ pint double cream
2 oz butter, softened

4 fl.oz dry sherry
2 tablespoons lemon juice
Salt and pepper
½ oz powdered gelatine

Set oven to 350°F or Mark 4. Lightly oil a 1 lb loaf tin or a salmon mould.
Place the salmon in a buttered, ovenproof dish with the fresh herbs and cover
with water. Cover the dish with kitchen foil and cook for 20 minutes. Leave
the salmon to cool in the liquid, then remove the skin and bones, but reserve
the liquid. Pound the salmon flesh until smooth. Lightly whip the cream and
fold into the salmon. Soften the butter and stir into the mixture together with
the sherry and lemon juice. Season to taste. Measure 6 tablespoons of the
reserved fish liquid into a bowl and sprinkle the gelatine on top. Set over a pan
of hot water until the gelatine has dissolved. Cool slightly and then beat into
the mousse. Spoon the mousse into the tin or mould and leave to set in a cool
place overnight. Turn out to serve.

Rhubarb and Orange Jam

The flavour of oranges makes a change from the ubiquitous Rhubarb and Ginger.

1 pint rhubarb pieces, cut small and pressed down
3 oranges   ¾ lb sugar

First cut up the rhubarb into small pieces. Peel the oranges thinly, cut half the rind into thin strips and discard the remainder. Remove the white pith from the oranges, then cut the oranges into thin slices, removing the pips. Put the orange slices, the strips of orange rind, the rhubarb and the sugar into a saucepan over a moderate heat and bring very slowly to the boil, stirring frequently. Continue boiling until setting point is reached. Pour into warm jars, cover and seal.

Farmhouse Vegetable Soup

A homely, thick and substantial potage.

1 lb carrots	**2 oz butter**
1 lb onions	**2 lb potatoes**
1 leek	**Bouquet garni**
2 sticks of celery	**1 pint lamb stock**

Salt and pepper

Peel and coarsely chop the carrots, onions, leek and celery. Melt the butter in a large saucepan and add the chopped vegetables. Sauté for 10 minutes, stirring occasionally, until the vegetables are soft. Peel the potatoes and cut into small chunks. Put the potatoes, *bouquet garni*, stock and salt and pepper into the saucepan with enough water to cover the vegetables. Bring to the boil and simmer for 45 minutes. Remove the *bouquet garni* and serve. The potatoes thicken the soup and may disappear into the liquid. The vegetables may be diced or finely chopped, using a food processor, if preferred.

Spratley Cake or Fly Pie

*A currant pastry cake, so-called because it is rolled out until the currants
show through, to look like sprats or flies.*

4 oz shortcrust pastry

FILLING
4 oz currants   2 oz butter   2 oz sugar (brown or white)
½ teaspoon ground cinnamon or mixed spice
½ teaspoon chopped fresh mint
Sugar for sprinkling

Set oven to 375°F or Mark 5. Grease a baking sheet. Roll out the pastry on a
floured surface to a rectangle about half as long as it is wide. Mix the currants,
butter, sugar and spice in a basin and spread down the centre of the pastry.
Sprinkle on the fresh mint. Fold over the edges of the pastry to meet in the middle
and seal the edges. Turn the pastry over and roll out until the currants show
through. Place on the baking sheet, brush with milk and sprinkle with sugar. Bake
for 20 minutes. Cut into slices when cold.

Pack-horse Bridge, Derwent Dale

Green Tomato Chutney

Making chutney is a good way to use up a surfeit of green tomatoes.

4 lb green tomatoes	1 pint malt vinegar
1 lb apples	1 level teaspoon mixed spice
1 lb onions	1 level teaspoon dry mustard powder
2 oz salt	1 level teaspoon ground ginger
1 lb moist brown sugar	1 level teaspoon cayenne pepper

Finely chop the tomatoes, apples and onions. Put in a bowl, sprinkle with salt, cover and leave overnight. Next day, strain off the salt liquor and put all the ingredients together in a large saucepan. Bring to the boil and simmer gently for 1 to 2 hours, stirring occasionally, until the chutney is thick. Leave in the pan to cool. When cold put into jars, cover and seal.

Lemon Cake

A lemon sponge tray-bake, covered with lemon topping and cut into slices.

6 oz butter or margarine   6 oz sugar (caster or soft brown)
2 large eggs or 3 smaller ones   6 oz self-raising flour
Rind of 1 lemon, grated finely

TOPPING
2 oz caster sugar   Juice of 1 large or 2 small lemons

Set oven to 375°F or Mark 5. Grease an 8 x 10-inch roasting tin. Cream the butter or margarine and sugar in a bowl until soft. Beat the eggs in a basin and gradually beat into the creamed mixture. Fold in the flour and the grated lemon rind. Spread the mixture evenly in the tin and bake for 30 to 40 minutes until springy to the touch and a skewer inserted comes out clean. For the topping, mix the caster sugar and lemon juice together and, while the sponge is still hot, pour the mixture over the top of the cake. Leave to cool in the tin, turn out and cut into slices.

Hartington, Beresford Dale

Pheasant Casserole

The beef dripping gives this dish its distinctive flavour. A lighter-flavoured casserole may be made using butter, cider and apples instead of dripping, red wine, carrot and celery.

2 pheasants	**1 carrot**
2 tablespoons beef dripping	**1 stick of celery**
1 onion	**2 glasses red wine**

Salt and pepper

Set oven to 350°F or Mark 4. Prepare the vegetables and chop them roughly. Joint the pheasants, using the breasts and legs only (this saves having too many bones to cope with). Heat the beef dripping in a thick frying pan and brown the pheasant joints. Remove from the pan and place in a casserole dish. Put the vegetables in the frying pan and cook for 2 minutes, add the red wine and bring to the boil. Pour the mixture over the pheasant joints, season and cover the casserole. Cook in the oven for 1 to 1½ hours until the meat is tender.

Moist Chocolate Cake

A filled chocolate sponge sandwich finished with chocolate glacé icing.

4 oz self-raising flour   3 oz drinking chocolate   6 oz margarine
6 oz caster sugar   3 eggs, well beaten   1 tablespoon hot water

BUTTERCREAM FILLING
2 oz margarine   2 oz drinking chocolate   4 oz icing sugar
Water or milk to mix, if required

GLACÉ ICING
6 oz icing sugar   2 oz drinking chocolate   Water to mix (approx. 2 tablespoons)

Set oven to 350°F or Mark 4. Grease two 8-inch sandwich tins. Sieve together into a bowl the flour and drinking chocolate. Cream the margarine and sugar together in a bowl until light and fluffy. Beat in the eggs, a little at a time, adding a tablespoon of the flour mixture to prevent curdling. Fold in the remaining flour/chocolate mixture and stir in the hot water. Put the mixture into the tins and smooth the tops. Bake for 25 minutes or until the surface springs back when pressed lightly. Turn out and cool on a wire rack.
Filling: mix all the ingredients together until smooth and light. Spread on one of the cakes and sandwich together. *Icing:* add the water to the sugar and the chocolate to form a thick paste and coat the top of the cake before serving.

Braised Beef and Mushrooms

Port wine adds richness to this simple casserole dish.

1 lb chuck steak cut into 2 inch pieces	2 wineglasses of port wine
1½ oz butter	½ teaspoon mixed herbs
½ lb small onions, chopped	1 bay leaf
1 tablespoon flour	Salt and pepper
½ pint beef stock or water	½ lb flat mushrooms

Set oven to 350°F or Mark 4. In a flameproof casserole dish, melt 1 oz of the butter and brown the meat on all sides. Remove from the dish and set aside. Melt the remaining butter in the casserole and cook the chopped onions for a few minutes. Stir in the flour, blend in the stock and continue stirring until boiling. Return the steak to the pan and add the port wine, herbs and bay leaf, and season with salt and pepper. Stir until boiling. Put the lid on the casserole and cook in the oven for 1½ hours or until the meat is tender. Slice the mushrooms and add to the casserole; cover again and cook for a further ½ hour. Serves 4.

Derbyshire Oatcakes

These flat cakes can be served warmed up in a frying pan with bacon and eggs, or with lemon juice and sugar, or toasted with a topping of cheese or with golden syrup.

**1 lb fine oatmeal   1 lb plain flour   1 teaspoon salt   1 oz fresh yeast
1 teaspoon sugar   2-2½ pints warm water to mix (approximately)**

**FOR A SMALL QUANTITY
2 tablespoons plain flour   2 tablespoons oatmeal
1 teaspoon baking powder   Water to mix**

Mix the oatmeal, flour and salt in a warm bowl. Cream the yeast with the sugar and add ½ pint of the warm water. Pour the yeast mixture into the dry ingredients and add the rest of the water, mixing slowly until a thin batter is formed. Set aside in a warm place until well risen, about 30 minutes. Grease a frying pan and pre-heat. Pour cupfuls of the batter on to the hot pan and cook like thick pancakes for 4 to 5 minutes on each side. The oatcakes will keep for 2 to 3 days.

To make a small quantity, mix the flour, oatmeal and salt with the water to form a thin batter and add the baking powder just before cooking.

Thorpe Cloud and the Entrance to Dovedale

Lemon Curd

Home-made lemon curd is so much nicer than shop-bought varieties.

Grated rind and juice of 3 lemons
4 oz butter   8 oz sugar   2 large or 3 small eggs, beaten

Wash the lemons and grate the rind finely. Put the lemon juice, grated rind, butter and sugar in a bowl set over a saucepan of hot water. Stir until the butter has melted and the sugar dissolved. Beat the eggs in a separate basin and add slowly to the lemon mixture, stirring all the time with a wooden spoon. Transfer to a saucepan and cook, stirring occasionally, until the curd thickens and coats the back of the spoon. Pour into warm jars, cover and seal.

Christmas Crumble

This is a richly flavoured fruit pie filled with mincemeat and peaches and with ground almonds in the crumble topping.

4 oz plain flour	2 oz Demerara sugar
2 oz margarine	1 lb mincemeat
2 oz ground almonds	1 medium tin sliced peaches
Glacé cherries	

Set oven to 400°F or Mark 6. To make the crumble mixture, sieve the flour into a bowl and rub in the margarine until the mixture resembles breadcrumbs. Stir in the ground almonds and the sugar. Put the mincemeat in an ovenproof dish, spread out and cover with the drained, sliced peaches. Reserve 8 peach slices for decoration. Top the dish with the crumble mixture and bake for 25 to 30 minutes until the crumble is golden brown. Decorate with the reserved peach slices and glacé cherries. Serve hot with custard or cream.

Ashbourne Church

Ashbourne Gingerbread

Gingerbread men were made and sold in country towns at Easter Fairs and autumn Wakes Weeks. Fashioned in moulds, they were decorated with coloured hats and scarlet or white sugar buttons. They can still be found for sale today in Ashbourne and the surrounding area.

8 oz self-raising flour	1 level tablespoon golden syrup
Pinch of salt	4 oz margarine
2 teaspoons ground ginger	4 oz soft brown sugar

Set oven to 350°F or Mark 4. Grease a baking tin. Sieve the flour, salt and ginger together into a bowl. Cream the syrup, margarine and sugar together a bowl, then stir in the dry ingredients. Knead the mixture on a floured surface to form a smooth dough. Form into a sausage shape, press into an oblong and cut into slices. Place in the tin and bake the slices until golden brown; approximately 30 minutes. Allow to cool slightly before removing from the tin. Some local recipes add a little grated root ginger and/or a level teaspoon of mixed spice.

Treacle and Oatmeal Drop Scones

Popular in the North of England, drop scones should be eaten hot spread thickly with butter.

2 oz self-raising flour	**2 oz medium oatmeal**
1½ level teaspoons baking powder	**1 oz butter**
Pinch of salt	**1 tablespoon black treacle**
½ oz soft brown sugar	**1 small egg, well beaten**

¼ pint milk (scant)

Sieve the flour, baking powder and salt into a bowl and stir in the sugar and the oatmeal. Gently melt the butter and black treacle together in a pan. Add to the dry ingredients and stir in, together with the well beaten egg and the milk. Heat a thick frying pan or griddle and grease lightly. Drop teaspoons of the mixture on to the pan; as soon as bubbles appear on the surface turn over and cook the other side.

Bakewell Tart

This version of the Bakewell Pudding is often preferred both for its flavour and texture.
The use of ground almonds makes the filling firmer.

8 oz shortcrust pastry

FILLING
Raspberry or strawberry jam   4 oz margarine
4 oz caster sugar   4 oz ground almonds
2 eggs, well beaten   A few drops almond essence

Set oven to 375°F or Mark 5. Grease a shallow pie dish. Line the dish with pastry and spread with a layer of jam. Mix all the other ingredients together in a bowl and spread over the jam. Bake for 20 to 30 minutes until the filling is set. A variation of this recipe uses 2 oz self-raising flour and 2 oz ground rice instead of the ground almonds.

Thor Cakes

Thor cake, or Thar cake as it is sometimes called, was baked and eaten in the autumn, for Guy Fawkes Day and for country Wakes Week when the fair came to the villages, bringing merriment and joy. This particular recipe comes from Wirksworth. On the farms the Thor cake was heavier, rolled out to 2-inches thick and baked in a greased and lined meat tin for about ¾ hour.

1 lb fine oatmeal
1 lb plain flour
1 lb Demerara sugar
2 oz candied peel
2 teaspoons baking powder

1 teaspoon ground ginger
1 teaspoon coriander seeds
1 teaspoon salt
12 oz butter, softened
1 lb warmed black treacle

Set oven to 350°F or Mark 4. Grease a baking sheet. Mix all the dry ingredients together in a bowl, rub in the butter and add the treacle. Knead together and roll out fairly thinly on a floured surface. Cut into large rounds, place on the baking sheet and bake until golden; about 20 minutes. The actual cooking time depends on the thickness and the size of the cakes.

The Shining Cliff, Middleton Dale

Eggy Bread

Egg-soaked squares of bread, fried and served with crisply fried bacon for breakfast or, on its own, as a snack.

4 thick slices white bread	**Tomato or brown sauce, to taste**
3 eggs	**Salt and pepper**
2 tablespoons milk (optional)	**Butter for frying**

Whisk together the eggs, milk (if required), sauce, salt and pepper. Cut the slices of bread into quarters. Soak each piece of bread in the egg mixture and coat well. Heat a little butter in a large frying pan and fry the soaked bread pieces until golden brown, turning over once. Any spare egg mixture should be poured over the bread as it is fried.

Meat and Potato Pie

In this steak and kidney pie, a layer of potatoes covers the meat before finishing with the pastry crust.

8 oz shortcrust pastry

FILLING
1 lb stewing steak and kidney   1 large onion, chopped
1 bay leaf   Salt and pepper   2-3 lb potatoes
1 tablespoon cornflour

Put the cubed meat, the chopped onion, the bay leaf and seasoning into a saucepan, cover with water and cook, covered, for 2 to 2½ hours until the meat is tender. Peel the potatoes and cut into 1 inch cubes. Put the cubes into a saucepan, add some of the stock from the meat with water to cover and bring to the boil. Cook for 5 minutes. Drain the potatoes and reserve the stock. Set oven to 375°F or Mark 5. Put the meat into a deep pie-dish, cover with the potatoes and moisten with stock. Roll out the pastry larger than the pie-dish and cut a 1 inch strip from around the edge. Place the pastry strip around the edge of the dish and then cover the pie, pressing the edges firmly together and trim. Make a steam hole in the centre. Bake for 30 to 35 minutes. Thicken the unused stock with cornflour to make a gravy, to be served separately.

Eyam Church

Wakes Cakes

Wakes Week was an autumn festival to cheer people before the coming of the long dark nights. Merry-go-rounds, hawkers, stalls with ribbons and gingerbread and of course Wakes Cakes. Each village had its own particular version of these cakes and some would flavour them by the addition of ground ginger, but this was never part of the basic recipe.

8 oz butter	½ teaspoon baking powder
6 oz white sugar	3 oz currants
1 egg, beaten	½ oz caraway seeds
12 oz plain flour	Grated rind of 1 lemon
	Sugar to sprinkle

Set oven to 375°F or Mark 5. Grease a baking sheet. Cream the butter and sugar together in a bowl, add the beaten egg and mix in all the other ingredients to make a firm dough. Roll out thinly on a floured surface, cut into rounds with a 2½-inch cutter, sprinkle with sugar and place on the baking sheet. Bake for 10 to 15 minutes until lightly browned. The 'cakes' should be crisp and sweet like biscuits.

Lemon Haze

A light, fresh flavoured sweet; a type of mousse.

**1 lemon jelly   ¼ pint hot water   Grated rind and juice of 2 lemons
4 medium eggs, separated   4 oz caster sugar**

Dissolve the jelly in the ¼ pint hot water and add the grated rind and juice of the lemons. Set aside until the jelly begins to thicken. Separate the yolks and whites of the eggs. Whisk the egg yolks with the sugar until light in colour. Add the jelly mixture and mix well. Whisk the egg whites until they are thick and stand in peaks. When the egg and jelly mixture begins to set, fold in the beaten egg whites. Pour into a glass serving dish and stand aside to set. Decorate with whorls of whipped cream and refrigerate until required.

Country Sweet Cake

This spicy fruit cake is also known as "Cut and Come Again Cake".

¼ pint milk
½ oz yeast
8 oz plain flour
4 oz butter, softened
4 oz brown sugar
4 oz sultanas

4 oz currants
¼ teaspoon bicarbonate of soda
½ teaspoon ground nutmeg
½ teaspoon allspice
½ oz ground rice
½ oz glacé cherries

A few drops almond essence

Set oven to 300°F or Mark 2. Grease and line a 7 x 9-inch x 2-inch deep baking or roasting tin. Warm the milk slightly and dissolve the yeast in it. In a bowl, rub the butter into the flour and add the rest of the dry ingredients. Mix in the combined yeast and milk. The finished cake mixture should be soft in texture. Put the mixture into the tin and bake for 30 to 45 minutes until the cake is set and a skewer inserted comes out clean. Leave in the tin for 10 to 15 minutes and turn out on to a wire rack to cool.

Poached Trout in Cream

A simple dish which enhances the delicate flavour of the fish.

2 trout	1 tablespoon water
1 dessertspoon chopped fresh chives	2½ fl.oz single cream
1 dessertspoon chopped fresh parsley	Fresh breadcrumbs
Juice of 1 lemon	Butter

Set oven to 375°F or Mark 5. Cut the fish from head to vent, gut, wash thoroughly and dry. Lay side by side in a buttered, shallow ovenproof dish. Place a knob of butter and a few of the herbs in the centre of the dish. Sprinkle the rest of the herbs over the fish and add the lemon juice, together with 1 tablespoon of water. Cover the dish with kitchen foil and cook for 15 minutes. Heat the cream in a saucepan and pour over the fish when cooked. Sprinkle with breadcrumbs and shavings of butter and brown under the grill.

Viator's Bridge, Milldale

Potato Cakes

*Left-over mashed potato can easily be turned into these scone-like cakes
to be eaten hot with butter at teatime.*

8 oz left-over mashed potato **2 teaspoons milk**
2-4 oz self-raising flour **Salt and pepper**
Butter

Knead the flour into the potatoes and milk in a bowl, using as much flour as can be worked into the potato to enable the mixture to be lightly rolled out on a floured surface. Cut into circles with a scone cutter. Lightly grease a griddle or thick frying pan (a wipe with a butter paper works well) and cook for 3 to 4 minutes on each side until browned. Serve hot.

Derby Sage Parsnips

Parsnip chunks are coated with local Derby Sage Cheese and roasted;
delicious with roast meats.

1 lb parsnips, peeled and cut into chunks
3 oz plain flour   1½ oz Derby sage cheese, finely grated
Salt and pepper   2 tablespoons dripping

Set oven to 400°F or Mark 6. Peel the parsnips and cut into small chunks. Mix the flour, cheese, salt and pepper in a mixing bowl. Put the parsnip chunks in a pan of boiling, salted water and bring back to the boil. Cover and cook for 3 minutes. Drain the parsnips and, while hot, drop a few at a time into the cheese mixture. Shake the bowl to ensure a good even coating, then transfer to a tray. Place the dripping in a roasting tin and pre-heat in the oven. When hot, remove the tin from oven and put in it the coated parsnips. Spoon the hot fat over the parsnips, return to the oven and bake for 35 to 40 minutes, turning over after 20 minutes. The cheese mixture will only coat the parsnips while they are steaming. To keep them 'steamy', drain only a few at a time.

The Great Court, Haddon Hall

Milk Bread

Serve this crusty bread at tea-time with butter and jam.

3 lb strong plain flour	**1 oz yeast**
4 teaspoons salt	**1 teaspoon sugar**
2 oz lard	**¾ pint milk**
½ pint water	

Sieve the flour and salt into a bowl and rub in the lard. Cream the yeast and sugar in a basin. Warm the milk and water together until tepid and add to the yeast and sugar mixture. Pour the liquid into the centre of the flour mixture. Mix to form a soft dough and knead for 5 minutes. Place in a bowl, cover and leave in a warm place to prove for 1 hour. Knock back the dough and knead lightly on a floured surface. Shape into loaves and put in greased loaf tins or on to greased baking sheets. Set aside in the warm to prove for 30 minutes. Meanwhile set oven to 425°F or Mark 7. Bake for 10 minutes then reduce oven to 400°F or Mark 6 and bake for a further 30 minutes. Remove the loaves from the tins or turn over, if on baking sheets, and bake for 10 minutes more to brown the crust.

Tangy Damson Mousse

A fresh-tasting dessert for late summer days.

½ pint damson purée
4 oz sugar, approx. to taste
1 lb cooking apples

½ block lemon jelly
½ block orange jelly
1 egg white

To make the damson purée, cook about 1 lb of damsons in a little water and with sufficient sugar until soft. Remove the skins and stones from the pulp. Peel and slice the apples and stew in a little water until soft, then dissolve the two half blocks of jelly in the hot apple purée. Mix together the damson purée and the apple mixture. Beat the egg white until stiff and fold into the mixture. Put into a glass serving bowl and leave to set. Serve with double cream.

Duffield Batter Pudding

Traditionally this fruit pudding would be made in a pudding basin which is sealed tightly, placed in a pan of boiling water and boiled for 1½ hours.

Fresh stewed fruit or a tin of fruit, as preferred
4 oz plain flour   1 pint milk   1 oz melted butter
3 eggs, beaten

Set oven to 350°F or Mark 4. Grease a shallow ovenproof dish and spread the fruit over the base; drain tinned fruit as required. Sieve the flour into a bowl, moisten with a little of the milk, stir in the butter and the eggs and gradually add and mix in the rest of the milk. Pour the batter mixture over the fruit and bake for about 50 minutes, until a knife inserted in the centre comes out clean. Serve warm with cream or ice cream.

METRIC CONVERSIONS

The weights, measures and oven temperatures used in the preceding recipes can be easily converted to their metric equivalents. The conversions listed below are only approximate, having been rounded up or down as may be appropriate.

Weights

Avoirdupois	Metric
1 oz.	just under 30 grams
4 oz. (¼ lb.)	app. 115 grams
8 oz. (½ lb.)	app. 230 grams
1 lb.	454 grams

Liquid Measures

Imperial	Metric
1 tablespoon (liquid only)	20 millilitres
1 fl. oz.	app. 30 millilitres
1 gill (¼ pt.)	app. 145 millilitres
½ pt.	app. 285 millilitres
1 pt.	app. 570 millilitres
1 qt.	app. 1.140 litres

Oven Temperatures

	°Fahrenheit	Gas Mark	°Celsius
Slow	300	2	150
	325	3	170
Moderate	350	4	180
	375	5	190
	400	6	200
Hot	425	7	220
	450	8	230
	475	9	240

Flour as specified in these recipes refers to plain flour unless otherwise described.